CRADLING TIME

Poems on Motherhood

ERIKA LYNN

mothers long to return to childhood
to remember simplicity,
to relive the fleeting moments of
laughter, learning, freedom;

grandmothers long to return to motherhood
to rear with the joy
they never could muster without the overwhelming tasks
of tediousness & self-doubt.

to my mother,
may these words
allow you to
forever cradle time

&

to rosamond grace,
i will always remember
you this way.

CONTENTS

THE GROWING PAINS

THE GROWING UP

EPILOGUE

ABOUT THE AUTHOR

THE WAITING

BECOMING MOTHER

do you know what eternity feels like?

it's fibers of life being woven inside you
like the spreading of time,
warming the oceans of your blood
within the lapse of a breath.

eternity is two cells, multiplied
by two hearts/souls
whose yearning
bent forward like a sphinx
forming out of ancient dust.

it's one waiting at the door,
peeking out of the window, losing her mind,
& one coming in slowly,
carrying grocery bags, talking nonsense.

it's one grabbing the other's hand,
pulling him madly to the kitchen,
to the table,
to the test,
to the sign of christly relics,

to the other side
of eternity:

the start of you.

SERMON

i know you are not a reward,
not a settled transaction
between a pleased god & a woman
who ceased to yield to the doubts.

you are the bread & the wine,
the manna for a journey that's only begun,
the person who has changed
my perspective on possibility.

perhaps you are, in every way: grace;
an opportunity to learn to be faithful,
to understand paths aren't always smooth,
but they are perfect.

because i knew life without you,
i knew the bleakness of tarrying
on rocky trails, searching for signs.

& now that i know life with you,
i know you are the greatest sermon of my life

because despite my hesitant heart

& mumbled prayers,
you came to us

& i've learned
that families form in so many ways,
but they all start with

undeserved
love.

SPILLING SECRETS

lips pressed tightly; humming through days;
clenching teeth; hiding syrup drips;
oh, the sweetness of it all.

sparkling eyes squint closed;
deep breaths & looser clothes;
oh, the sweetness of it all.

heart bursting
like overfilled balloons; like rushing rivers;
oh, the sweetness of it all.

each word spoken feels like an invitation;
each glance an invocation;
each time my mouth opens,
i'd like to mention,
to share, *the sweetness of it all.*

lips pressed tightly;
humming through each day;
each young child i pass
becomes my own;

until my heart,
bursting like overfilled balloons,
like rushing rivers,
spills the secret to a stranger
like
honey
dripping
from hives
on a
warm day.

MY CRYSTAL BALL

the pink line,
now
the size of a blueberry
inside my womb/heart is
utterly dependent
on me.

so no caffeine, no beer,
check the ingredients,
no deli meat.

natural makeup, natural deodorant,
natural shampoo, organic foods.

living only on
lemon ices, preggie pops,
ginger ale, pretzels.

living only on
his grin, my prayers,
this strange secret
& baby apps.

is that raw egg yolk in that dressing?
was that dip pasteurized cheese?
what does *momof3* say about herbal tea again?

i believe in god, but
google has become my crystal ball.

everything is so new/quiet &
i need answers/help
because you're inside
my womb/heart
& you're
utterly dependent
on me.

ULTRASOUND

though i've only seen you in black & white,
you are my sun,
             my moon,
                   my stars:

the world spins madly on,
yet you are ever-fixed in my mind.

        i carry you,
but really,
it is you who carries me.

i can feel you move,

                        twist,

             kick,
                      shake,

but still
        i love to see you
suspended in this stillness;

you remind me to

       s l o w   d o w n

because
it's already been weeks
      since you were this
              small

& if i blink again

i'll miss the moments
when you need me the most.

STRETCHING

the tightening
          begins
                  with
                      the muscles
                              the tendons
                                      the skin

                                              looser pants
                                              &
                                              softer shirts

                                              all of
                                              the parts
                                              of me

                              making room
                          for you

                      making room
                  for all my

              love
          for you

BLUE OR PINK?

blue like crisp plums &
hometown football jerseys.

blue like storm clouds & rain,
like robin eggs & neptune.

like denim & tanzanite,
peacocks, blue corn & blue crab.

blue like the crystaled tapestry
of our favorite waterview escape.

blue like the shadow
of you on the ultrasound screen.

pink like cotton candy &
spring cherry blossoms.

pink like winter cheeks & grapefruit,
like erasers & sugary lemonade.

like seashells & rose quartz,
flamingos, peppermint & piglets.

pink like the warm afterglow
of our backyard skyline.

pink like the kissable face
we imagined you with

& blue like our tears
when you showed yourself,

because all of earth's colors
came rushing in all at once
& *loved* is what they painted.

A QUILTED LIFE

when you look
upon your nursery quilt
i hope you know that

   each piece was
   stitched purposefully,

      according to design,

like you were

   by the master artisan.

   & as you age,
   when you see the many parts
   of yourself,

      i hope you love them all,

because in your self-love,

   they become complete.

THOUGHTS WHILE WASHING CLOTHES

with gentle soap on gentle cycles,
i gently put your clothes away for the first time,
tucking & folding each little arm & leg,
wondering how the fabric will feel
wrapped around yours.

there are few quiet moments like this,
but when they come, i blink:

suddenly, i am six & downstairs in the playroom,
dressing dolls in little smocks & little hats,
making crying noises
just so i can rock them asleep again,
just so i can sing my mother's lullabies to them.

now, when i hold your sock,
it's only the size of my thumb.
i can hardly fathom that
your feet will fill them.

i have always been a dreamer,
but i've never known how to let dreams
live outside of my mind.

but i'm alone in your room
& i'm learning that when it's real,
it doesn't feel like it.

it's god's way of startling our imaginations,
letting us know:

yes, it is a miracle,
yes, it is mine,

feel it with your whole heart.

CAR SEAT INSTALLATION

in a few weeks,
maybe a little less/little more,
you will arrive,
bringing
all of the light/magic,
all of the glimmer/hope
i've felt inside me.

little one, when you are ready,
we will take you home.

being your first,
this will be a trip
i will forever remember.

one day i will replay
how your father & i put in
your car seat, knowing
we were
your first tour guides
& that our lives would be spent
showing you the wonders of
this life.

we were bright-eyed & hopeful,
on an adventure,
knowing you were ours & we were yours.

our first journey was home/together
& from that day forward,
we will forever journey that way.

THE WAITING

it's been leggings & pineapple,
spicy foods & pressure points.

your father tinkers on his motorcycle to bring it to life
& prepares for your long naps by greasing the door hinges.

your dog watches over your empty swing & sighs,
trots the perimeter of the yard,
barks at every out-of-place leaf

& follows your mother,
who walks & walks & walks
because this has been a journey & maybe
the strides & the swaying of her hips will invite your arrival.

the house has become quiet,
the silence leaves us performing these rituals of anxiety.

there is something missing without you.
we miss you without having seen your face,
without having grasped your tiny hand;
we miss you as we miss a part of ourselves.

today we heard your heartbeat again &
it rang with joy & possibility:

you are our new year.

& though we endlessly walk/pace—
thinking about how we want you to see
the trees, the houses, the sidewalks
with your own eyes—

we've known from the beginning
that you will choose your own time
& we love that about you.

BILLOWS OF PAIN

get some rest;
                sleepless, anxious.

no, you can't eat;
                weak, starving.

but you can shower;
                the contractions, the cramps,
                i can hardly stand the pain.

      they didn't tell me this,
      no, my body never imagined this,
      the foreignness of it all.

      the beeping, the lights,
      the endless entrances & exits.

      the nurse is here again to check.

nothing yet.
      she smiles, marks on a chart.
      she's gone & i can't speak to him
      except to ask for
            more ice, more water,
            more chicken broth,

>   the only things that keep
>   my body/spirit from giving up.

how are you feeling?
>   crying, wincing.

you're in that much pain?
we can give you medicine;
>   you can? *yes. yes, please.*

let me inform you of the risks...
>   they go on for minutes,
>   each getting more painful, but
>   i cannot worry more than i have already,
>   it cannot be worse, worse than this.

you cannot move — okay?
>   *okay.*
>   i am a stone.
>   though the pain comes
>   in billows now,
>   i do not move.

do you feel better?
>   i become warm,
>   my legs leaden,
>   the blue cotton gown heavy,
>   the waiting, heavier;
>   the seconds, burdensome.

>   the nurse is here to check again.

how do you feel?
> strange.

do you feel anything?
> something.
> it's not pain, but pressure;
> it's not misery, but movement.

> *oh my god.*
> *oh my god.*
> *oh my god.*

> it's you.

THE ARRIVAL

BREATHS THAT TAKE YOUR BREATH AWAY

i didn't remember the breathing i'd practiced,
nor the harrowing minutes turning into hours,
when tears clouded our eyes &
the astonished nurse summoned the doctors;

you were ready to take your first breath.

my breaths — once scattered, drifting —
now fixated on three.

one.
two.
three.

your father gave me his hand,
the only thing he could do,
but
i couldn't squeeze it.
i let go to

p u s h —

all of my strength i sent to you,

p u s h ing, p u s h i ng, p u s h i n g,
imagining all that was mine becoming yours,
as i do when i take communion & think
his blood is now mine, his body, my own.

one.
two.
three.

p u s h —

six times to get from the
crown of your head to your tiny shoulder
& by the seventh,
your hand;

your hand.
the first thing i saw
as the doctor
placed you on my chest,
skin covered in white vernix,
eyes wide,
feasting on the moment,
mouth open,
gulping in your world.

i didn't remember
the breathing i'd practiced,
but as i held you, looked at you
pink & breathing new world air,
i inhaled then exhaled.

the one breath that mattered the most
ended on three:

you, me, daddy.

HERE

you were
a white blanket & hands & closed eyes,
your head tilting towards me;
everything about you seemed so small.

i studied your face,
memorizing it,
the way i will memorize
your every word & deed &
will trace in detail,
in coffee shop conversations & christmas letters,
how you've grown,
how you are making your mark
on this big, wide world.

your father took you, held you bare-chested
— so securely you slept —
your heart resting on his,
& i thought about how
he'd already figured out the secret to fatherhood:
letting his heart teach yours,
showing you the steady rhythm of love,
letting you learn what he has discovered

over the course of his lifetime.

when your grandparents arrived,
they cried, laughed, fussed over you;
two from the south, two from the north,
four speaking the language of their unconditional love,
simply for you being born,
simply for you being yourself.

they held you like a prize &
it was so clear:
we will always remember this first day,
the day we learned you are more than
we could have imagined.

today until forever, we'll remember watching
you become yourself for the first time
& then witness in wonder as you grow up
into even greater versions of yourself.

FALL RISK

your grandparents, your aunts,
your uncles, your cousins,
have all held you,
have all doted over you,
have
        all gone.

i sent your sleep-deprived father home to our bed
& to take care of the house, the dog, himself.

it's me. it's you.
it's quiet. it's dim.

it's the first night & i hold you,
wrapped in your swaddle,
as if you are a part of me.

the band on my wrist says
        fall risk.
the nurse comes in & cuts it off,
as if i have passed a timed test
& leaves.

you cry & cry & cry
& i want to ask her to come back, to stay,
to take you, but she's
a nurse, not a babysitter
& it's the first night of your life
& i am your mother
& i should be a better one, i think.

your eyes haven't closed since the earth welcomed you
& the night has brought a ravaging hunger,
a yearning that brings a well of tears from your eyes.

i try to feed you, to warm you,
to gently move you, to lull you to sleep,
but you are helpless against
the stark change in your world.

all you do is cry & cry & cry &
my eyelids are falling, falling, falling
& i tell myself: *don't, don't, don't.*
you'll drop the baby; the baby will get hurt;
it will all be your fault; *wake up.*

i get out of the bed but
i'm so tired, so weak, so overwhelmed.
all of the bravery & the optimism & the resolve
has dwindled with the fleeting light.
i hold you, wrapped in your swaddle,
as if you are a part of me, but i feel like i'm falling,
        failing already.

i blink & the minutes fall into hours,

the darkness into light
& we tumble out of this first night
like two weary warriors.

HOME TOUR

your dad holds your car seat,
steadying it like an egg on a spoon.

he drives the speed limit,
checks the mirrors, his blind spots & your tiny face.

he keeps the music off, snuffs out prolonged conversation,
takes no risks, tries no shortcuts, just drives.

it's our first trip home as a family & we keep
telling you all of the people & things that await you:

your dog, your books, your crib,
your backyard, your blankets, your sidewalks.

we enter the house quietly, afraid to wake you, except
your eyes open at the sound of your dog's nails clicking on the
floor.

we tour you around your house, show you your room,
the one we spent hours imagining, designing & creating.

your grandma snaps a picture of us.

later, we look at it.
it's us:

a family who is home,
a family who is together, &
a family who knows how careful we must be.

SETTLING IN

how can it be
that i've known you forever,
yet only days?

how can it feel like you've walked beside me
my whole life?

it must be that you have god in you:

your hushed sighs are prayers,
your gaze tells of
angelic visions.

you are proof of miracles
in more ways than one,

for in your tiny hands, your small feet,
you are evidence of the generosity of a god
who walks among us in human form.

ORGANIC, ALL-NATURAL FIVE-HOUR ENERGY DRINK

i never knew sleeplessness
could be so refreshing.

my heavy eyes shoot open,
my drunken feet become chariots
my numb mind thinks sharply of you only.

your whimpers, your sighs,
your purring & your cries,
they all speak in familiar tongues,
beckoning me to come alive.

i thought i needed more rest,
but the truth is i only needed
your heartbeat to wake me.

you have taught me that the next moment
is always imminent
but it's never promised &
so i wake for you & i study your movements.

i look for the shadow of your face, for your cap in place,

i listen for the whispers of your breath
& i feel for the coldness of your hands.

last night i thought i needed
more hours to rest,
but the truth is, i only needed
your heartbeat to wake me
to the wonders of the night
& the poetry of insomnia.

i never knew sleeplessness
could be so refreshing

& i never knew skipping clocks & slipping hours
could light up the soul.

TO HIM, THE OKAY MAKER

when the cries have lasted all night
but the night ends in the blink of an eye,

he wakes up slowly as to not
break the suspended silence in the air;

he lets the dog out & feeds her;

he eats breakfast & comes upstairs to dress;

he whispers *good morning* to me,
hiding blurry eyes & a fatigued mind
with a toothy smile that never seems to fade.

the baby cries again.
he picks her up—
she looks so small in his arms—
& gives her a tiny kiss on the forehead,
saying *it's okay* as he rocks her.

though he is talking to her,
i feel like he is talking to me,
because he always knows what to say,

even when he doesn't mean to.

my eyes have seen a thousand ways
that he makes everything okay:
like the glowing dawn
breaking through the blackness.

FROG POSES & SAFE HAVENS

it's your frog pose,
i say;
curled up & nestled against
my chest,
ear pressed to my beating heart,
legs tucked in tight as if you
want to disappear.

you were across the room in your swing,
wrapped in a blanket,
whimpering;
maybe you're scared of being alone
or maybe things are just better together.

but you quiet in this spot on my chest,
as you hear my voice, feel my warmth.

burrowed deeply, your
ear pressed to my beating heart,

i never imagined being someone's safe haven
but here i am, yours.

WEEPING TUNDRA

there have been seven days of
frigid air & clouds hovering over the house.

you were fussing; our dog, bored,
was waiting by the back door, whining.

i thought i'd lose my mind so
i wrapped you in a fuzzy blanket
& turned the knob.

the first step out was freedom,
a surprising, pleasant warmth.
by the second,
your cries ceased & you became serene.
the winter sun kissed your face
& the crisp wind caressed it.

though you could not speak & hardly smiled,
i recognized the feeling that flickered in your eyes.

the dog stretched & meandered;
i stood looking out at the trees,
then to you, my wide-eyed, fresh-faced one.

i told myself to remember this moment,
because it was a miraculous one,

one where a little child who has never
welcomed the sun after days of cold,
has recognized its beauty, its gift
& basked in it.

everything is new to you, a first.
i hope you'll always have these firsts:
unexpected, beautiful, meaningful

& that you'd remember this first lesson:
darling, there will be cold, but there will be sun, too.

COSLEEPING

you woke up every two hours,
tossing, turning, tossing again;
you were a jungle that night.

by morning light,
your father kissed you on the forehead
& it lingered until he left for work.

the tiredness wouldn't leave me
& your restlessness stayed,
so i took you from your bed
& snuggled you next to me.

your eyes turned half moons,
your breath, smelling faintly of milk,
became a whisper;
your arms fell to your sides
& you nestled into my ribs, completely still.

for three hours,
we stayed suspended like that,
me, half awake, careful not to move;
you, melting into sleep, silent.

i took a photograph
to show your father your ways,
but also so i would
remember the nightly struggles
that led to mornings like this:
where dimness hovered over us
& we hid under the covers,
warm.

SHOTS (WHEN THE NEEDLE PRICKED YOU)

you're two months old,
ten pounds & ten ounces,
twenty three inches tall &
growing out of something each day.

you look at me, at your father
& you really look.
you follow our movements
& miss us when we step out of view.

you tell us this,
speaking the language of god,
unintelligible utterances to everyone
except for whom the message is intended.

we now know your tones,
your body language, your facial expressions
& what they all mean:

hands to mouth, tongue out &
a sudden cry if you're too hungry;
short "ahs" when you want to be changed;
a quivering lip & long wails when you long for sleep;

a sharp, painful scream when your tummy hurts;
shrills & babbles when you are content at play;
& silent stillness when you are engaging with your vast world.

*

you had your shots today;
the sound was one i'd rather not recollect/know,
but it was the same bellow as on your first day of life
when a needle pierced your heel
& your father & i learned the lesson about
 seeing your child in pain:
you wish it was you who felt it instead.

today, when the doctor was done,
we gave you a bottle;
you quickly forgot the pain, the bleeding.

you came home & played
& looked at me & spoke to me
as if it was any other day.

but as you slept, i held you,
not wanting you to sleep anywhere else,
knowing it was not like any other day

because i remembered your innocence
when the needle pricked you;

i thought you'd break
& that the pain i couldn't take away
would make you resent me,

but in my arms
your sweetness still lingers
& when you wake, your hopeful eyes
still look at me
— really look.

i am grateful how already your strength astounds me
& how, already, all the pain i cannot take from you,
you have conquered on your own.

ERRANDS & MELTDOWNS

i strapped you in your car seat
with an idealistic sense of purpose,
journeying to accomplish a to-do list a mile long.

we were hardly down the road
when your coos became whines,
your whines became cries.

i changed plans to suit your mood,
deciding to go to a closer store,
then missed the light & sighed.

i turned up the nature sounds,
but they didn't calm your anxieties;
my shoulders tensed,
fingers strangling the steering wheel,
as your cries became incessant,
until
they became wails,
became hysterical,
became inconsolable,
until
i turned around to go home,

surrendering my plans &
repeating *it's okay* for the hundredth time while
holding my finger out to remind you i was there.

only minutes from our house,
your sobs came from the deepest place of sadness,
so sad, so deep, that i felt they came from myself.

pulling into the garage, i
opened the car door to scoop you up,
realizing my most important errand was you.

i unstrapped you from the carseat,
your lip trembled
& your pitch rose high
as if you were trying to get the pain out of you.

i lifted you to my face, tears in my eyes
& held you as i walked around the house,
telling you over & over that it was okay,
that i love you.

you finally grew quiet,
but my eyes could not stay dry
as i realized this was what it meant to love someone:

that their tears become your own,
that the lists dissolve
& nothing is more important
than to hold them as they crumble into sleep.

THE GROWING
PAINS

ANXIETIES OF A (FIRST TIME) MOM

the things i don't write about enough
are the tentacles.

questions unravel:
forming, pulling, choking.

are you breathing
becomes should i call the doctor again
becomes
will i wake up to you gone—erased even?

almost everything becomes existential this way,
no problem is surface-level, marred by circumstance,
everything is growing from the inside out.

is there enough time between work/home/life
becomes would quitting this afford me more hours
becomes
will i ever have enough time to love you?

what should you be eating by now
becomes whose advice should i trust
becomes

do i even know what's right for you?

are you laughing enough
becomes are you happy
becomes
do i even deserve you & your joy?

there are so many more tentacles these days:
straining, snaking, spreading.

my thoughts become lap dogs
to these tendrils,
relish in them even.

anxiety is the shadow,
the outline
& for a lifetime
i've lied to myself saying:
life becomes deeper this way,
more complex,
more meaningful, even.

even if i can't breathe,
even if i can't convince myself
to remember the truth.

sometimes the tentacles hold onto me,
but, i,
i too,
hold onto them,
comfortable in their embrace
—not breathing.

when it's quiet &
you're asleep on my chest,
i look at you inhale,
so pure,

when you exhale,
so alive,

inhale,
so mine,

exhale,
so loved,

& as you continue,
for as long as you do,
i believe that i can shed the tentacles.

i know life is meaningful without them

i know i can forget the questions,
let them slip from consciousness
as quickly as they entered,

but it requires the elusive faith
that lives
beneath the questions.

it requires the faith of a child,
the miracle of the divine breath.

& so i ask:

with each breath,
teach me.

GRABBING

you're four months now
& you reach for our faces,
hold our cheeks in your hands
& open your mouth wide
while your eyes squint half moons.

you grab
my hair, my sunglasses,
your toys, your bottle,
the reachable world before you.

anything you can hold, you love.

you have a joy that is magnetic,
already people gravitate towards you,

you ignite smiles,
laughter,
a warmed heart,
just by watching,
just by playing,
just by breathing.

you reach for our faces,
take ahold of our world
& we are full of joy because
anything you can hold, you love.

TO FATHERS WHO HANG THE MOON

you may never remember how almost every morning
he woke with the sun,
wiping the dew off his shoes
to lift weights,
but one day you'll tell stories about
how his strength held up your world.

you won't recall the hours he beautified our home,
but you will run around the yard,
imagining the rose bushes are dragons,
that the shed is your very own playhouse,
that magic lives any place draped in carolina sunlight.

you'll forget the business trips & FaceTimes,
the dinners out where he made his appearance
then rushed home to see you asleep,
but one day you will meet these strangers that worked with
your dad
& they will tell you how he talked about you incessantly;

they will tell you tales of your own babyhood
& you'll know you are his inspiration for everything.

you may never know that while you slept,
he read/wrote/studied,
but one day when he sits with you to do math homework,
you will know that you can always improve,
can always learn,
can always be proud of growth.

you will see the pictures of you both together,
laughing, smiling, joyful
& you won't remember why,
but you will say that he has always been
the funniest, most exuberant, loving &
dedicated man in your life.

you will remember your dad,
the one who hung the moon—
even when you didn't know it—

& even as you grow old,
you will see the luminescent glow in the darkness,
knowing that you are the star of his sky
& that you always will be.

MOVEMENT

like a corkscrew,
        you twist your body out of the swing,
nuzzling yourself into the pillowing like a mole,
        believing that if you push enough,
                you'll come out on the other side
if we would only let you try a little longer.

&, darling, you roll;
                roll,   roll,   rolling
                over & over & over
across the floor until you get stuck,
                breached where the carpet meets the hardwood
                or limbs wrapped around your playmat arches.
                but even when you're tangled,
you're holding your head up like a prideful seal,
calling out for help like you know it's coming.

                this week,
            against couches & chairs,
            you try sitting up to pose
        for presidential portraits with gummy smiles,
        the only member of the paparazzi being mama.

you have learned to flip & flop
in your crib;
you love to cozy up to the sides &
stick your arms & legs through the slots,
trusting that adventures await
in any tiny space that opens to you.

even though we
scoop you up from your burrowing into the swing &
put you in the playpen to keep your rolling at bay &
put mesh bumpers around your crib &
hover near the couch to keep your body from slouching/
sliding,

we love to watch
you explore your vast world;

we only want to
protect your spirit.

so keep being brave,
brave child,

but
also know

we will always come for you
when you cry for help.

REMEMBERING DALÍ

you were strapped to my chest,
eyes wide & focused on
dalí's enigmatic paintings,
a pacifier strung from
your bib to your lips
& your bald head tucked under my chin.

it was a quiet place,
paintings in rows &
bodies in sacred poses,
eyes filled with contemplation & remembrance
of a time & world
before (or after) the present.

the drooping clocks & hidden figures
spoke to me:
the mystic, the ephemeral,
the ancient, the symbol,
the surprise within the familiar:
it all made me look twice.

the silence was broken
by your sudden whines,

whimpers, shrieks, screams:
your mouth became a rebellious hymnal.

rushing out, i hushed you,
feeling the glances of
surrealists & security guards,
tour guides & tourists,
suddenly aware & wondering if it was a faux pas
to bring an infant to an art exhibit.

a man in a blue suit jacket & earpiece
approached me as we exited.
i panicked,

but he smiled
asking if we needed a place to sit.

he brought us back through the exhibit,
darting the inquiring glances,
& into a nook, a paintingless place of solitude.

your bottle quieted your stirring
& as you ate,
i thought about how the night before,
as you fell asleep,
you smiled,
then let out a light laugh.

i thought it was because you were seeing angels,
dancing, ancient, swirling shapes,
maybe you could see beyond,
maybe you could remember heaven's gates.

among the disjointed faces & floating forms,
you finished your bottle with eyes fluttering &
i smiled,
thinking about how when you
saw the chaos
of the paintings,
you remained still,
as if you were remembering
a time & world
before (or after) the present

until it made you sing.

TASTING THE WORLD

he said i was more important than
water, because you lived on
my milk
alone.

it was the most poetic thing he'd
ever said, besides *i love you*.

*

on the floor, you put feet to gums
as if to taste
the earth

& at the table, you study
our mouths & the food
that moves from fork
to teeth
to tongue
to gone.

*

we want you to taste
the world:

the tangy, tartness of grapefruit,
the cold, bittersweet of cranberry sauce,

the salty lingering of a pretzel & the creamy
sweetness of icing that drizzles over it,

honeyed barbecue sandwiches, peppery potatoes,
savory green beans, mellowed banana pudding,

papaya & curry & pupusas & chile & bisques,
bagels, beans, basil, blueberries, biscuits.

because
you didn't need water,
for
i was once everything you needed
to live,
but now
i want to show you that the world is vast,
colorful, savory, lush, appetizing.

so i
will give you crisp water with a hint of lemon
& every combination of pizza that fancies you.

i will fix you a plate,
i will widen my palate again,
so you
can taste the world,
one bigger than i ever knew,
so you may know that this world is good.

SEPARATION AT 1:45 AM

i want to be on the floor,
legs to chest inside an oversized t-shirt,
rocking like i used to as a kid.

it's 2:23 am, you awoke
38 minutes ago, shouting in your sleep.

i put your pacifier in your mouth,
you fell deeper into your dreams
& i am awake realizing the month
i have been avoiding has closed in,
hovering over the future like
the second hand on ticking clocks.

i thought something would have
changed the course by now,
a harbinger, a savior, a path,
but it's only been days on calendars
forcing us closer to being apart.

each day i remind myself to be present;
to enjoy the diaper changes & stained bibs,
to embrace the toys strewn across the floor

& to know my purpose:

soothing cries & making you laugh,
catching your head before you topple over,
feeding & rocking & loving & watching you grow.

but the present has a heaviness,
a suffocating richness like
mountain air;
it's all too meaningful,
too much, even

& you've come from our ribs,
so every breath you take, i feel.

i want to stay here with you,
to see all of the wonderful things
you do with that breath &
to hold you when fear or excitement
takes it away,

but it's august first
& in eighteen days i will try to sleep again,
knowing that the next day you will nap in a different crib,
be fed by a stranger's hand,
play with toys i will never clean up.

i keep thinking it's a dream &
i wait for the day that i don't wake up
feeling the burden of the gift & breathing the
warm, sticky air of holding onto summer.

i keep waiting for something,
a harbinger, a savior, a path,
to change it,

because, you come from our ribs
so when we are apart, i feel it —the severing —
jabs & pangs & tears at the corners of eyes.

& i want to be on the floor,
legs to chest inside an oversized t-shirt,
rocking like i used to as a kid,
practicing a primal reaction to stress:
movement & closeness,

but instead i breathe,
because one day i'll understand that
growing up is painful for us all
& i will always miss you this way.

MATERNITY LEAVING

on & off you slept on me
while i wrote lesson plans,
wondering what lessons
i'd miss giving you while i was gone.

i've fought spontaneous tears for weeks,
thinking about not being here to
snuggle you into a few more hours of sleep
or to welcome your wry smile
that wakes with you & the sunrise.

i've spent nights imagining your confusion
when daddy gets you ready each day
because i'll have to sneak away
in the early mornings & hope you'll sleep a few more hours
just so you don't realize i'm gone longer than you have to.

*

in the afternoon haze, i've felt
the weight of boulders on my chest
as i look at you sleeping peacefully,

because there are times when the only way

your tears stop is when i tuck your head under my chin
& hold your body against my chest
just so you can hear my heartbeat.

*

at dinner my throat tightens knowing
you watch me from across the room
& hold my fingers in your hands
& use all of your strength to orient yourself closer to me,

but, still, i'm leaving you.

*

i pray for you every night,
that you will understand,
that you will know somehow:
this is the hardest thing i've ever done.

*

i already miss our strolls in our lonely neighborhood,
feeling the sun's gentle warmth
& seeing your squinting eyes
as the stroller wheels click on the sidewalk.

i miss our slow mornings & fussy nights
& changing you eight times before lunch.

i miss the desperate conversations
you start with me using babbles & shrills

& i miss the bubbles that form on your lips
as you sit in your rocking swing observing the world.

i miss knowing that you don't have to miss me,
because i'm always there when you need me.

but most of all i miss you,
the person who you are,
without even leaving yet.

*

i'm scared of what i'll miss,
i'm terrified of what i can't get back,
but, i am trying to be brave,
because one day you'll have to be brave too

& the moment i became your parent,
i signed up for a lifetime of learning how to let you go.

SNOTTY COVERS

your eyes are droopy marbles,
your nose a cold plum,
your cheeks blanched & mouth open
as if welcoming air through a door.

symptoms started after
five days of daycare,
five days of work,
five days apart;

my heart feels it as a
metaphor.

                    *

you aren't the only one
with a snotty nose & misty eyes.
i, too, pull into work,
wipe mascara into place,
cough to clear my throat,
take an extra inhale to invite air.

i want to turn around, pick you up,
give you my shirt sleeve to wipe

your nose,
rock you to sleep for an extra long nap,
follow you with tissues as you crawl from toy to toy.

but instead, for dinner,
we choose foods with vitamin c,
push water & saline wipes,
put you to bed early with the humidifier hissing;

your father buys homeopathic droplets
& lets you sleep in as long as you'd like
& he relishes his mornings with you.

*

at daycare, your teachers are kind
& through watery eyes & snot,
you make it through another day &
smile with delight
when i pick you up in the afternoon.

though this has been hard,
maybe harder than i imagined,
the moment you felt unwell,
you called out to us in the night:

wailing & wet-nosed,
you wouldn't fall asleep until you
were nuzzled in our arms.

you slept in between us that night,
as if to say,
now i can fall apart,

now i can be held together,

& i will always thank you for that.

FEVER DREAM

you wouldn't fall asleep
in your bed, nor mine,
so i rocked you in the chair
until you closed your eyes
& now i'm afraid to move.

it's been months of sickness
& the numbers feel endless:
  the phone calls, doctor's visits,
  doses of medication,
  the bills & copays,
  the missed work days,
  the multitude of ways
  we've felt that your small body
  has had enough.

i don't know how many times i've
cleaned the entirety of the house,
only to remember the germs are invisible,
that as i scrub they may even be
conjured in my mind,
but as you sleep, wide-mouthed,
once again feverish & sad,

i feel your spirit in this sleepy silence:
      it is still
      & it is resolute
      & it speaks of life,
      saying *i'm fighting this —*
      over & over —
      i am still fighting this.

when you wake,
we put on music;

you clap along with a weepy guitar
& smile your fever as though everything
is just a dream.

HANDS FULL

lunch is done.

in the overcrowded dishwasher,
where bottle tops rest over spatula handles,
i shift coffee mugs to make room for your bowl.

i splash water on a paper towel & fight
you to clean your face & hands,
the latter of which you are so possessive over
that i can hardly remember them grasping my thumb.

i go upstairs to change you
into your third outfit for the day

on the narrow staircase,
we descend
step-by-step
with the dog slinking
next to us, you on my hip,
juggling the laundry basket
on the opposite side.

     you reach, wiggle, grab,

the dog's fur bristles against me,
i'm bobbling the basket — you —
& i startle myself by thinking:

if i lost my balance,
if we were to fall,
which would i grab first?

because on weekends every task seems priority,
every errand breathes urgency,
every detail demands attention
like carrot stains
on a white onesie.

THE WELL-MEANING

the well-meaning said:
    it will get easier;
    you'll value your time together;
    you'll feel worse than she does.

but it's been months
& it isn't easier.
    i'm tired enough to pawn
    you off on your dad
    or relinquish the present
    to tidy dishes/my email inbox.

    i still fight tears every morning.
    you still don't nap enough at daycare
    & you melt into tears when i pick you up.

but i am overly cordial to your teachers,
i bring them tissues, sweets, kindness & cards.
i smile when i see your father & talk about
my day as if reciting a grocery list.

    in the afternoons,
    i put you down for a late nap &

i think i'm finally learning:

maybe it gets easier because
you push back the emotion,
look for the slits of light,
coast through your day;

you get used to living halfway present
& become okay with it.

& maybe this is why i weep for every mother, everywhere.

THE GROWING UP

YOU

it started when you'd fuss.
i'd carry you around the living room
showing you family pictures like
we were at a gallery opening.

i'd repeat the name of each person
as every good docent would,
explaining every location/situation/nuance
like i was critiquing the paint strokes of time.

you love the picture of daddy & i:
we're laughing in the back of his truck,
newly engaged, wild-eyed & burning for the future.

i point to myself smiling into the sky &
put my hand to my chest saying, *mama,*
tap my index finger on the glass
to your father, whose arms wrap around me,
saying, *& dada.*

next to ours is a picture of you.
i put my hand on your heart, repeating your name
to cement the image/sound of yourself

so you never forget who you are.

weeks later,
you pull yourself up to stand & pound
palm to heart,
beating on your chest as if
to tell me *that was me, i did that.*

& i think, *yes, baby, you did,*
until you again rest your hand beneath
your dimpled chin,
feeling the pulsing of being alive
as if to say,
this is me, mama. see, it's me.

THE WILDEST THING

you started scooting on your
dad's thirty-first birthday
& you pulled yourself up from floor to ottoman
on your aunt's thirty-fourth.

your father & i looked at
each other, mouths wide,
terrified.

*

in the morning you wake
between 5:30 & 6.
after nursing, i try
to get you to sleep next to me
for a few more minutes—

it never goes well.

you flip & sit & roll & spit raspberries,
you grab my hair & flutter kick my stomach,
you bury your head into my pillow & shriek
& i am tired, but i laugh & roll my eyes,
because how can i complain?

you are our gift.

*

changing your diaper/clothes
requires at least two adults
& a barrage of toys & noises
& still you turn,
grab the table's sides,
howl & whine at the injustice
of temporary stagnation.

this morning, i've flipped you
over six times & want to yell,
but i remind myself to sing
because it suspends even the wildest things.

*

when people casually ask
about your schedule, i freeze.

my mouth can't convey your patterns in times/numbers,
so how can i explain how i care for you except to
say my ears know when you're hungry,
my arms feel when you're indignant,
my eyes can tell when you're worn,

because there are no boxes for you, my dear.

we can't keep you still;
you were born alive,
fire burning at both ends,
current fast,

a comet against the black,
spinning dizzy like crop circles.

*

i used to write poems as you slept on me,
stomach to chest,
with time suspended until feeding,
but this morning you crawled across the room,
eyes locked, smile spreading,
just to welcome home your daddy.

your father & i looked at
each other with wide eyes,
entranced,

knowing you are our volcano:
free,
effervescent,
always waiting to burst.

PICTURES OF YOU

i take too many photos of you.
you've learned the art of posing,
you flash a gummy grin whenever
you see the phone in my hand.

you:
face pressed against the
aquarium glass glow;
yanking your dog's toy away;
squirming next to your cousins;
holding a teddy bear in a wagon;
squinting as you sit on a bale of hay.

even the blurry ones, the ones
with my fingers cropped in the corner,
i know i'm going to want to return to
them one day.

when you're slated to graduate,
i'll pull them out over & over again;
you will roll your eyes at me,
because i've always had
a flair for poetic nostalgia.

but one day,
i hope you'll look at
your messy face,
your father's steady feeding hand
& that you will remember
me,
the one behind the camera,
the one who couldn't let the moment
pass too quickly,
who had to capture it,
because these are your memories,
but i can't help but believe
they're mine too.

ON EXISTENTIAL CRISES & BEING MYSELF

last night i asked him if there
were parts of him that he missed,
that have disappeared:

the selfish ones.

*

i had driven home alone
to music i knew every word to,
notes that raised me/lyrics that made me create things,
wondering if i was still that person.

because there are moments i miss,
moments of aloneness,
of reading stories &
writing memories,
of living inside of music
& of feeling on fire.

*

but he said,
he's exactly who he is
meant to be,

& i believed him.

despite his dreaming mind,
he was never for wishing away
the present,
of struggling with what if?
or maybe should...

to him
uncertainty is only possibility masked;
it's for bending with the future,
not contemplating the present.

*

& because of him,
the music is still there;

i write some & read less
& when i forget myself,
my guiding light
reminds me:

>the future comes
>with a
>miraculous fury,
>
>so
>lean
>with it.

BABY BOOK

this morning i awoke to the realization:
five years ago i finished
the first draft of my first book.

i remember the rush of
being in it,
of really handing myself over to the muse.

like the caffeine from each drink
sipped at every cafe table
& like the pulse of the subway station,
the words & worlds coursed
through me,
made me alive even.

*

this morning i also awoke to the realization:
you slept through the night;

it was the first time
i wasn't awoken by murmurs
or your whimpers.

over breakfast, i watched you
turn over your basket of toys,
sifting to find the one you wanted,
until you tried desperately to inch
towards a book.
as if to say, *i, too, am captured.*

*

later you pulled up in your walker,
a red car that makes you look
like a carefree teenager,
then reached with palms up to tell me
you wanted me to hold you while
i made my lunch.

i picked you up & told you
a story about a mom
making herself eggs
because it was the only thing in the house.

& while you napped for an endless two hours
while i packed for your second trip of the summer,
put in laundry,
washed bottles & bowls,
& thought about how
my compulsions have changed
to the material.

*

as suds disappeared down the drain,
i think about the stories i'd write,
but i don't get the rush of being

consumed by them anymore,
of living in them as they
break the stitches of reality.

instead, now, there's a fullness,
a feeling that warms from the inside out.

alive is different, it's serving
this muse who grows in a million
different ways in each moment
& my imagination explores
all of the ways i can bring magic to you.

still,
i write to capture your stories
in moments when I can find the words/the time
because though i miss the rush of creating a new world,
i love to live in yours & each day
i love waking up to become your historian.

FINDING YOUR FEET

it doesn't matter that you wobble some
or that you have to take head-first dives
into our laps/arms to keep from wiping out.
your legs are brand new,
your feet, the greatest toy ever invented
& there's nothing we can do to stop you;

you've been reborn.

we hover, giving you our index fingers for balance &
preparing our palms to catch your head,
but you've shed your timidity
& conquer the underworld of the kitchen table,
parading between chairs like you're on a tightrope.

your pigeon toes & bowlegs
motor around the living room
not to find anything in particular,
just to move, to shift space, to ripple time.

in the car/stroller/shopping cart,
you tear off your shoes any chance you get.
but on the couch as i pull up your socks,

serenity drapes over you & you wait ever so patiently
as i stick your shoe on & adjust the tongue,
knowing they are your gateway to the great backyard abyss,
that with them, the world will open for you.

to watch you is a beautiful, bittersweet vision of growing up
because the moment you found your feet,
you tried any path they could wander—
the uneven grass, the stone, the rubber, the concrete—
you travel across them, treading so buoyantly,
falling like you are a part of the earth.

you find yourself: the person who could/would
go wherever their heart leads them.

FIRST WORDS

your words are syllables that stumble,
s k i p like records;
they are bubbles BURSTING forth
into static air:

ma / ma, ba / ba.

ba / ba / ba / ba / ba / ba.
ma / ma / ma / ma,

then,
          suddenly:
                    DADA?

said with inflection/purpose,
at least that's what i told your father.

                    *

you're pushing twelve months
& each morning
your teeth awaken,
your tongue energizes
& your lips tremble to move air,

to form words,
to be inhaled like a desperate breath

because words are the way to the divine.
that's the way back to babel.
& as hours age you, it seems,
your soul more vividly
recollects & orients towards these
ancient remembrances & primal compulsions.

*

the dog barks outside.

you put fingerprints on the back door, repeating:

dah. dah. dah. dah.

you call to the hurricane of fur
that wiggles around you,
wiping your face clean
of all traces of breakfast,
as if to say:
i know your language, too.

*

one day you'll be speaking sentences,
maybe delivering speeches,
but, for now, i wait for your growing syllables.
they are like buzzing molecules,
like atoms crashing into each other,
like ions scattering, like towers falling:

shifting, dynamic, teeming.

i listen for the meaning breaking
its way into my bones,
sourced from a heart desiring to give voice
to oneself,
to reach the whole earth,
to learn its language
& to build a tower to god.

A WISHFUL SIPHONING OF YOUR MEMORIES

i once heard a nation's politics
is a child's childhood.

*

i told your father that i
can't imagine being a mother
where bullets scat across
abandoned streets,
where walls crumble to feet,
where hunger pangs don't
last hours, but days.

i look at you pulling yourself up,
not on tottering fences or make-shift gravestones,
but on plush couches, rubber toys — & me.

*

i never want the terror to touch you,
not a lick, not a scrape,
not a lingering scent of war
to come close.

you are far too innocent,
too sweet & too wonderstruck
to ever know what sorrow feels like.

*

terror isn't a part of you yet
like it is me.

it was one day, like many,
that started with the sun.

then there was fire;
the walls collapsed,
the wallpaper tore,
the picture frames splintered
& the smoke lingered for weeks.

the terror still haunts me,
but for the first time in years
i think this:

my father's eyes witnessed far more
than i could have ever known/survived;
he bore it to protect us, but
none of it makes sense,
which is why the anguish comes
out a little at a time.

*

i worry about the politics of today,
how it will sway your memories,
but the terror is what i worry about

the most.

one day, you also may remember
fire & smoke & glass & walls,
but i hope you don't see it all,
that you don't feel it all,
that i, or your father,
can protect you

because the only broken glass you should see
is from a shattered glass ceiling;
the only fire, from inside your soul;
& walls shouldn't crumble,
except through a shy glance, a soft touch;

for you are too innocent,
too sweet & too wonderstruck
to ever know what sorrow feels like.

RAISING/BEING A DAUGHTER IN AMERICA

sometimes you cry out in the middle of the night
& i want to scoop you up &
save you from the terrors of your own mind
but you are strong & you are courageous.
you wrestle them yourself & fall quickly into a peaceful sleep
while i stay awake, thinking how
there are so many shadows waiting for a young girl.

*

it's 2 am & i scroll insomnia away,
only to see ted bundy's ghost
resurrected for entertainment
& though
violence against women should not be entertainment
nor a subplot to a grandeur story about a man,
&
i haven't watched lifetime in years,
these familiar plotlines stick with me:

it's dangerous to be a woman,
to be alone can be a death sentence,

you are never safe,

even/especially in america.

*

as a girl, i don't remember ever going to the bathroom alone.

as a teen, i grew to walk through parking lots,
keys between my fingers, white-knuckled & vigilant,
locking my car as soon as i got in.

in college, away from my parents/siblings/cousins,
the rules of survival became a fat book with tiny print:

> *don't drink with people you don't know,*
> *don't trust the boys you do know when they've had too much*
> *because what happens next could be hard to swallow.*
>
> *don't be too pretty, dress down/blend in,*
> *don't make eye contact, look mean/confident/disinterested/taken,*
> *don't dance like that,*
> *don't flirt/speak*
> *& definitely don't leave with anyone.*
>
> *don't go into taxis/ubers/lyfts unless you're with a friend*
> *& even still, pay attention to your driver/location/license plate,*
> *keep your phone charged/always with you/with location services on,*
> *share your ETA*
> *& don't forget to look behind you when you get out.*
>
> *don't fall in love blindly, be careful who you let in,*
> *they may be the worst thing that ever happens*
> *to you/your ability to feel safe*
> *with yourself/within yourself.*

*

over long distance calls, my mother reminded me of
the tragedies of being a woman
& made me promise not to wander the mountainside alone;

i look back to those suffocating years of
being so desperate to be untethered/safe/loved,
to experience moments of exploration/existence/regeneration,
that, still,
i'd go to the woods.

though i reacted to every cracked twig,
every shift of the wind
& carried a knife the size of my forearm,
i was alone;
    alone, overlooking the valley & reading philosophy;
    alone, jogging rocky trails to free myself;
    alone, basking in the sunlight & the silence;

    alone, being myself in front of nobody.

*

i almost never leave you alone.

i hate to drop you off anywhere with anyone, because
when you vanish from my eyes it's as if you vanish forever.

when i'm unstrapping you from the carseat,
i peer around, two, three, four times & once more.

you've started running/hiding from me, & my breath flees;

i see now how fear & anger intertwine in an instant.

my mother & grandmother still send me news articles
about kidnappings:

slow drivers passing schools;
strolling/lurking along walking trails;
phony religious solicitors at the door;
internet grooming & seduction;

each time i want to shatter the screen
because i'm exhausted.

*

being/raising a daughter in america means
so many conversations start with
    don't
    &
    be careful

& i look at you & all i want to say is
    do.
    do whatever you want,
    when you want,
    with who you want
    &
    don't be scared of this world.

i don't want to have to teach you to say
    no,
as if it is a tool of survival as unnatural as physics.

i want your words to have enough weight to
mean exactly what they mean
without walking on eggshells,
without masking your intentions,
without it being taken as a challenge
that must be conquered.

because
i have nephews,
& maybe you will have a brother one day,
& they must all know this:

silence is not a yes,
but a chance to ask a question,
to let a girl speak her mind freely,
to listen & learn from her words
that breathe her goodness,

because that is love,

& a woman's love can change
your world/the world

& we all need that chance.

NEIGHBORHOOD STROLLER GANG

your neighborhood best friend is here.

like cherubs, you speak shrilled slurs &
both hover over a plastic stroller, entranced
by the sharing of a thing.

your cloth baby is pulled out of its safe haven
& cast aside on the floor,
only to be picked up/hugged again by the sensitive soul
who is your first friend.

her fingers, still clumsy & small,
are unable to tuck the baby in again.
still you start pushing the stroller away, empty.

maybe i miss seeing that sweet doll snug in the stroller,
or maybe i miss your eyes being that small &
me as your only fixation,
but i insert myself into your play, reminding you that
the cloth baby is on the ground.

you squat to recover her

then push her slouched body into the stroller,
giving her a pacifier.

you stride away from me
& your diamond-eyed friend
crawls behind with a glowing smile.
you glance back to make sure she's still there,
your cheeks dimple from your widening grin.

the letting go happens in so many ways,
but if it must, i want it to be this way:

witnessing you bask in the warm fullness of companionship
& knowing there are some loves i can't give you
but only
pray for you to have.

YOUR EYES (THE ONES THAT SEE WHAT I CANNOT)

the first thing i noticed about you
was that your eyes were not the same as mine,
not the color nor the shape.

they didn't match your father's either;
they were your very own.

you saved us an argument;
the one where were we claimed
the parts of you that we believed
belonged to us.

for that i am thankful
because there are many parts of myself
that i hoped you wouldn't inherit & many
parts of your father that i prayed you would.

but staring at your beautiful, beautiful eyes,
i found they looked like pools of water:
dark, still, yet tense,
on the brink of movement.

your gaze made me believe in god,
as there is not an ounce of me that could have
created the masterpiece that you are.

you came into the world as your very own
& as you age, i hope you know that about yourself.

*

as you grow into yourself,
i will try to see things your way,
but you will see things that we will not
& you'll want to take a closer look.

so i want you to know, my darling,
that gaze, well, that is uniquely yours
& i've always loved that about you.

there are many paths you can take
if you're willing to travel alone.

so go.

don't be scared of them—even if i am—
for you will inevitably make your way out of the woods
having seen many wonders along the way.

all i ask is that you make sure you capture them
for me
for your father
for others—
as we very much wish to see with your eyes.

ONE UNTIL INFINITY

before your first birthday party,
a woman i knew told me that
she once wondered why americans
threw such extravagant first birthday parties—
with the themes & the cakes
& the guest lists a mile long—

but when she had her son,
then she understood.

having a child who
survived the first twelve months
is a blessing, she said.

i, too, conceded with that thought,
however dark it was,
because the burden of eve's knowing
grows with me as i age
& as you age.

the stories of lost children have stalked me for months.
they come with a swipe, a scroll, a headline, a text, a mention:
they are readily waiting for me each day.

sometimes they stick to me like
the shadows beneath your eyelashes.

most of the time,
i push them away, hard,
because i don't want a grip on you that
you cannot break when you're ready to.

*

on the day of your first birthday,
you wore your crown proudly around the house,
as if you knew that your life was worth celebrating.

you smashed your
overpriced birthday cake
& fretted over the frosting
slathered over your arms & face;

i laughed & tried to feed you some
knowing your life is immeasurable,
your happiness is contagious,
your goodness is a promise kept to us all.

*

when the party ended & every crumb
was cleaned up,
i looked at the pictures of your day,
promising myself that,
despite how quickly this strange world moves,
on each birthday/milestone we will
stop time to do the things you love,

the things that bring a toothy smile across your face.

because
time does not exist in our hearts,
instead it's filled with these moments of you,
suspended, yet alive—
like poetry—

so when we celebrate,
it's not in fear of losing you,
but in the joy
of having you,

our one-year-old going on infinity.

CRADLING TIME

we pray before dinner.

you hold my hand
with tiny fingers, squishy palms
& a joy that grows from
your smile to your eyes.

you hold on well after
the prayer is done,
glancing back & forth
sheepishly;
it's a game to you,
one that you are still
figuring out the rules to.

when we finally let go
to bring forks to mouths,
my hand becomes cold,
missing yours.

*

in the morning,
while i empty the dishwasher,
you rove around the kitchen.

legs stretched, toes curled inward,
your belly leads you,
poking out
like a kind old man's.

you duck under the table,
hover beside the trash can,
child-pose on the floor mat.

your shoulders slither into the pantry,
you shred napkins,
pick them up between thumb & index,
then hand me the tiny remnants.

                    *

i dry another bottle— sometimes i feel
trapped here, thinking about the many
hours i've spent in this exact spot,
cleaning/drying/moving things.

but then you scamper into the living room to play your piano &
it's a cacophony of high notes & primary-colored lights &
suddenly,
i am thankful for this spot where i can summon
a montage of the many stages you've grown
through already
because

soon enough, you'll pinch my knees to
be picked up.

soon enough, you'll be scarfing down

a bagel over your math homework.

soon enough, it will be an empty table, crumbless,
with beautiful placemats & too many seats.

*

i tuck you in each night.

at times, when i cradle you,
i can feel the sands of time
falling right through my fingers.

i tell myself to hold onto this:
the ocean waves rolling through the silence,
your eyes glistening in the dark,
your body still (the only time all day).

because you still drink a bottle,
but the milk disappears quicker than it used to
& you push me away when you
want to dive into sleep

& we miss you each night so
we watch you on the monitor,
feeling your hair lengthening,
knowing each morning you'll wake
a bit older

& we talk about you until our eyes close,
trying to relive the day that passed too quickly,
holding onto you in our words,
like cradling time.

EPILOGUE

HOW TO BE A MOTHER

give me quiet,
give me movement;

give me natural & alone,
give me a moment of peace;

give me a floating, white cloud
& a steady blue sky;

she gives & she gives,
this mother of ours,

so give me remembrance of
beauty & power,

of a mother that does not tremble
at the sights of man,
but blossoms in the night,
sprouting life from ashes.

& though my insecurities/frustrations
grab/pull like currents/webs,

though my dry throat gasps for air &
i reach for words like light switches,
i no longer raise my fists to god, questioning.

because along a river,
i found myself, standing still,
breathing/seeing
the mother in me emerging from the river,
bold & beckoning,
revealing that certain things are planted/permanent;
that all that ebbs, flows;

& all that flows,
returns to its source.

ABOUT THE AUTHOR

Erika Lynn is a mother, wife and writer born and raised in Long Island, New York. She holds an MFA in Writing for Children from The New School and a BA in English Education from Covenant College. She lives in the Carolinas with her husband, daughter and their dog. This is her first collection of poetry.